A Walk Through Darkness

ALSO BY CLARA RUTH HAYMAN

*Protecting Alabama: A History of the
Alabama Environmental Council*

*A Judge in the Senate:
Howell Heflin's Career of Politics and Principle*
(winner of the 2002 Clinton Jackson Coley Award)

A WALK THROUGH DARKNESS

For All Those Who Grieve
And All Those Whose Grief Is Yet To Come

CLARA RUTH HAYMAN

MBF PRESS
Montgomery

MBF Press
105 South Court Street
Montgomery, AL 36104

ISBN-13: 978-0-9785311-5-7
ISBN-10: 0-9785311-5-9

Design by Randall Williams
Printed in the United States of America

Life

"Shall we dance?"
asked the wind.
"Oh yes, yes!" gaily
replied the leaves.
And so the wind swept them up,
lifting, turning,
tip-toeing
over the earth.
His breeze lifted them
high into the air—
swirled them 'round—
intermingling from one to another.
As they finished their dance,
they snuggly settled down.
And then he kissed them
ever so gently.

CLARA RUTH HAYMAN

Contents

Acknowledgments

A Walk Through Darkness would not have been possible without the help, love, and support of a lot of people. There are so many family and friends who have been there for me through this grief process – so many more than I deserve and way too many to mention. However, I would especially like to acknowledge the following persons who helped me directly with this book.

Heath Bowen, who read the manuscript from the standpoint of one who deals with death on a daily basis. His position as a funeral home manager gave me another perspective to consider as I worked on this book.

George and Judy Jolly, my friends and stockbrokers who have been so patient in dealing with me and my finances and who read my manuscript to make sure my financial advice was sound.

Gorman Jones, what do I say about the best and most caring physician? Not only did Dr. Jones take care of John but he has taken good care of me. He has exceeded any expectations of a physician, including the reading of and commenting on this manuscript.

Malcolm Marler, my confident and friend, who made sure I stayed "on track."

Sarah Shelton, my minister, who pursued her dream/calling of being a "preacher" while bravely battling the prejudices and bigotries against women in religion. She conscientiously read the manuscript, made comments, and urged me forward.

My Sunday School class—Connie and Dave Bowers, Javin Bowlin, Michael Brogan, Jeff Hairrell, Lawrence Hughey, Cathy Kelly, Patsy Love, Max Martin, Suzy Goggans, Becky Belcher, and Charles Dorris. Unknown to them, they provided much discussion and feedback to my ideas, questions, and search for direction.

Ann Robinson, the best friend one could have for thirty years. She lent a caring heart, listening ear, extreme loyalty, and utmost profession- alism to all my work.

Randall Williams, my publisher and friend, who not only gave me emotional support with this book, exceptional feedback and editing, but brought this book to fruition.

And most important of all is Nancy Jo Doran Shutt, my sister, who was the inspiration for this book. She listened to my ponderings, my questionings, my lamentations, and, yes, even my jokes about my experiences. She shared her own experiences with me, guided me, and suffered with me. She insisted that I put everything in writing, and she provided excellent ideas, feedback, and editing. She has always been my support and my trailblazer in this world. I cannot imagine life without her.

Introduction

Imagine if you will, life as a large jigsaw puzzle. Laid out in front of you are thousands of small pieces to be placed in their respective spot and to be interlocked with the surrounding pieces. You pick up one piece, sure that it is going to fit—it looks right—has the right shape—and no matter how hard you try, it just does not fit. You put that piece down and try another. You continue with the trial and error process, sometimes having instant luck but at other times, seemingly, you have to try every remaining piece, until one day, the picture begins to emerge. The core of the puzzle is apparent, and you realize it is only a matter of filling in a space here and there to make the masterpiece complete.

One day, just when you seem to have only a few pieces left to insert, someone comes along and knocks the puzzle onto the floor. The pieces scatter, and the crucial piece of the puzzle is lost. Now what do you do?

The puzzle is an analogy to my experience when my husband, John Hayman, Jr., died, and six and one-half months later, my mother died.

I was comfortable with the way my life was going. I was happy. However, with these deaths, my life lay broken and scattered, just like the puzzle. The persons to whom my life was interconnected were gone—those pieces eliminated from my picture forever.

Since that time, I have gradually tried to pick up the remaining pieces and put them in order, trying to create a new picture. Existing puzzle pieces have to be evaluated to see if they still fit, some pieces have to be trimmed or reshaped, and new pieces have to be designed and cut. But, slowly, the new design is taking shape. It is a more abstract and spontaneous version of the old one. I have no clear picture of this new puzzle; it remains a mystery. The original model of family, friends, career, and such is no longer valid. At this stage in my life with both parents and my husband deceased, the changes are magnified and directions less clear. My physician tells me I am like a new version of Microsoft being developed, and he is very much interested in seeing the new me. So am I!

Interestingly enough, when my father died suddenly of a heart attack in 1966, I was in college and had never had a "close encounter" with death. Two of my grandparents were deceased prior to my birth, and my paternal grandfather died when I was only nine. Other family members had died, but they were not part of my daily life. I was very close to my father, and his death was a cruel blow to me. I was angry. I was hurt. But at that time, I did not understand, acknowledge, or really express those feelings because I came from a culture that said, "Suck it up, and get on with things." There was no one to counsel me, no one to help me explore and express my feelings. My mother was experiencing her own grief— privately, I might add. She did not discuss her sadness or loneliness or hurt with me. I went back to college and resumed my normal activities. The grief stayed locked away inside, but would exhibit itself from time to time in outbursts directed at my mother. In retrospect, I wonder how I could have hurt her so much when she was hurting so much already. Then I think, "If she had shared with me and allowed me to share with her, maybe these clashes would not have happened."

I was also raised to believe that if one is a Christian, death is not to be grieved. You just rely on God and everything will be okay. God will see you through. I no longer believe that Christians or anyone for that matter have to put on a front, suck it up and go on, and be so strong. Grief is something that reaches out, grabs, and holds. Grief is normal. Grief hurts. Grief is raw. Grief is hard. Grief is hell. It takes every bit of one's strength and resistance to wiggle out from its clutches. And, in the midst of all this struggle, grief needs to be experienced and shared, and the griever needs to be supported.

As a result of this stoic, puritan background, I think I never really grieved for my father until John and Mother died. By this time, I was mature enough to acknowledge the deaths and grief, and to allow me the liberty to deal with them.

This book chronicles my experience in dealing with death and grief.

It was written to help fill the gaps I found with other grief books which seemed to focus either on the spiritual or the clinical sides of grief. My experience demonstrated that the grieving process is not an "either/or" process but involves the tangled web of all aspects of our life. Each aspect has to be dealt with individually, and, subsequently, collectively.

The book is an easy-to-read, honest look at my walk through the darkness of grief and the struggles I faced during the process of rebuilding my life. Individual chapters deal with the financial, mental, emotional, physical, social, and spiritual aspects of dying and grief. Included are suggestions of what to do before you or a loved one dies, what to do when death occurs, what business to take care of afterwards, and steps to take to make your changed life one that is meaningful and good.

It is hoped that every adult will read this book in preparation for facing death, whether their own death or the death of a loved one. It is also hoped that this book will provide solace and support for the ones already grieving, and that the suggested ideas will help those who are dealing with the bereaved. Perhaps others can learn from my mistakes and experiences, and this book will ease some of their stress and tension during difficult times.

This book is *not* intended to be a clinical dissertation or an authoritative manual on grief. It is, instead, one woman's experience from the heart. I am placing my heart, my raw emotions, and my experiences in the open for you. Perhaps knowing what someone else deeply and truly felt and experienced will let you know that you are not alone, and through death and grief, all of us have the pieces of our puzzle interlocked.

I

Is It the End . . . or the Beginning?

It was a chilly, rainy, October Saturday night. It was about 11 p. m. , and John and I were sitting in an examining room in the emergency section of a local hospital. We were laughing and joking about John's needing a "tune-up," trying to cover up the seriousness of the situation.

For a couple of weeks, John had been suffering from asthma complications. He was on high levels of steroids and had been in the hospital twice since August, most recently about a week prior to this event. As with past times, we figured it was just a matter of getting his medications correctly adjusted.

This Saturday was somewhat different. John had struggled to breathe all day. He repeatedly gave himself breathing treatments; I gave him hot broth to drink. John was weak, so we sat together in our bedroom all day—he in a low-upholstered rocker, I in an old-fashioned wooden rocker facing him. The steroids had caused swelling in his feet, legs and arms, and his arms were leaking body fluids. I had his feet and legs elevated and in my lap rubbing them. We had the television on for diversion. I read him the newspaper.

Twice I had called our physician, at home with the flu, to get instructions. Both times he suggested I take John to the hospital, but John refused. Finally, as we were getting ready for bed, John relented. So here we sat in the emergency room of the hospital.

Tests were performed and breathing treatments were given to try to stabilize John. About 3 a. m. on Sunday, he was moved to a regular hospital room. I went home to shower and to get a few hours sleep.

The next week was full of ups and downs. We went from one treatment to another, one test to another, and a battalion of doctors took their turns at examining John and giving their opinions. Our physician was still battling the flu, but was receiving daily reports.

Though I was feeling very apprehensive about this ordeal, several of the doctors assured me it was going to be okay; a solution would be found.

I went home at night, on John's insistence, but arrived very early each day and stayed until late. Then, we got bad news/good news. It seemed that John had developed blood clots, which caused him not to respond well to treatment. However, the doctors assured me that blood thinners would control this problem. So, we began additional treatments and tests. I say "we," because I was involved in all the decision-making processes.

Things continued downhill despite the new treatments, and I began staying at night. I went home long enough to shower and to change clothes. About the middle of the week, I had finally gotten John to agree to let me notify his children that he was in the hospital. I was giving them daily reports.

Saturday, one week from our arrival at the emergency room, things changed dramatically. John really began to suffer in trying to breathe. The oxygen and breathing treatments were not helping. Uncharacteristically, he began begging for something to calm him down, saying he was very tense. Of course, that was only a symptom of the real problem. The doctor-on-call was reluctant to give him a strong sedative because of his heart. What was finally prescribed barely helped. The suffering became more intense. Watching his terrible suffering actually made me sick at my stomach. There was a time I did not know who was in the worse state—John or me. I knew I had to be strong, but I was literally falling apart.

Finally, the doctors decided stronger medication had to be given. At last, John calmed down and slept. One of the interns insisted I get some fresh air and take a break. I did not want to leave, but she promised to sit with John while I was gone and to call me if a change occurred. It had been two days since I had been home, so I agreed. While home, I sent everyone emails about John's being worse. Since it was very early on Sunday morning, I called our minister and alerted him to the situation.

Sunday, several people visited. Two of John's close friends from out of town came—fully aware, I am sure, but not wanting to admit—this was their last time with him. Becky, one of John's daughters, arrived.

Sunday night, Becky insisted she stay with John while I get some sleep. Reluctantly, I agreed. However, sometime during the night, she called and said John was being moved to intensive care—not to worry however, this was just to assure that he got closer care. That did not fool me. I rushed back to the hospital in time to be with him as he was being moved. After he got into his new "cubicle," Becky left.

Reality began to swirl around me when both the nurses and the intern asked if I was sure I wanted to adhere to John's wishes as expressed in his living will. Perhaps it is the law, but this is such a cruelty toward family members. Fortunately, John and I had discussed our personal desires often and at length with each other and with our physician. We had signed our living wills and expressed our wishes on our respective forms. I knew John wanted no heroics. I also knew that if heroics were performed, it would just bring him back to suffer all over again—an action I could not justify.

As soon as 9 a. m. arrived, I called our physician's office, and told his secretary I needed him right away. She told me he was already on his way.

He came into the intensive care waiting room with open arms. We stepped outside and I said, "You have always been open and upfront with us. Now, tell me the truth." He replied, "Clara Ruth, I have been in to see and talk with John. If there is anyone you need to call, do so now. He is not going to make it. I have told the nurses to let you stay in the room with him." He also saw my own emotional and physical state and asked if I needed any medication. I refused.

I immediately started shivering—was so cold my teeth chattered. I could not get warm. Becky made the calls while I sat with John. Edie, John's other daughter, arrived later in the day. Friends came by.

The vigil on Monday night was agony. John's breathing was sporadic and very labored. One moment I thought he was gone, and then, the breathing would resume. About 5:30 on Tuesday morning, the vigil ended. John's breathing became slower, shallower, and further apart until the last breath was gone.

So—that ended my life as I knew it—and began what I knew not. Little did I realize what changes in my life would be made by that one single breath.

2

'Cuse Me—Where's My Brain?

John's last breath came slow and easy. The chaplain was called and John's two daughters and I were whisked into another room—four plain white walls containing a conference table with chairs stacked around the room. Not exactly a warm, comforting environment. We were asked if John was an organ donor (he was, and they harvested his corneas). I suppose the chaplain had a prayer and said words of comfort, but I really am not sure. I do remember she walked me outside to get some fresh air and to talk.

A discussion followed as to where to take the body. At least I knew that much! We were told to go home and to call the selected funeral home later in the day to set up an appointment for making the necessary arrangements.

A few days prior to his death, John had been told that he would have to be on oxygen after being released from the hospital. Not a pleasant thought to either of us, but I reassured him that a lot of folks maintain a "normal" lifestyle while on oxygen, and we could, too. A tank had been delivered to his room, and I had received instructions on its use.

Now, at the edge of daylight, I found myself walking out of the hospital into the brisk autumn air, carrying John's personal items and pushing an oxygen tank, which had to be returned to the provider. I was in a daze. It was only some months later that I realized the extent of the daze. I was freezing and shaking, not from the cold but from shock. Never in my wildest dreams did I ever think I would be a widow at my age or at this time of my life. I drove home feeling like a lost puppy.

Always, it seems, if I want things to go well, I keep my house clean and in good order. As sure as I am into some project and the house is a mess, some trauma will occur. John's death, and subsequently my mother's death, were no exceptions. Our house was in disarray from some remodeling. There were a few things left to do, and you guessed it, John died.

It was too early in the morning to call the contractor, so I began to arrange furniture and to do a little cleaning. I think I took a shower and tried to lie down to rest. It was useless. Finally, I called the contractor, told him my story, and he came and finished things.

Becky did all the calling of family and friends. I just wandered from room to room, and then people started coming by.

Later in the day, I called the funeral home to make an appointment to discuss arrangements. When my father died, I was either not included in the funeral arrangement decisions or have absolutely blocked that experience out of my mind. I was totally ignorant in this particular type of decision-making responsibility. Upon my questioning, the funeral director told me what I needed to bring with me.

Fortunately, I knew where the important papers were kept and our choice of burial clothes. For those of you who also are inexperienced in these matters, a list of what to do before, during, and after the funeral is included in the appendix. Now is the time to start working on that list.

The next few days were a blur. Strangely, I cried very little. I felt strong and in control, but at the same time, I felt like a robot going through the motions. Family members arrived and friends dropped by. Visitation, burial, and memorial services were planned and attended. There were many things to do and other people to comfort. Our physician told me later that I was the "ultimate Steel Magnolia." I am not so sure. I think I was just running on automatic.

I have read, and I believe, that the one(s) closest to the deceased should take care of as many of the details surrounding the death and burial as possible. Handling these matters is a first step in accepting the reality of the situation and is the beginning of healing.

John died on a Tuesday. The funeral service was Friday. Everyone was gone by noon Sunday. I think Sunday turned out to be the longest and most difficult day of my life.

I had insisted everyone leave and get back to their normal routine. I knew that eventually I would have to do the same, and for me, the sooner the better. It was not easy, but I come from a long line of strong women, and I was not going to be a wimp!

When the last car pulled out of the drive, I was still in my gown and robe—in which I stayed the remainder of the day. I went upstairs to our bedroom, took John's photo in my hands, and for the first time the tears truly overflowed. My body shook from the sobs and tears. What in God's name was I going to do now?

3

Taking Care of Business

Monday morning did not come early enough. I could not sleep, which was to become a nightly ritual. I kept asking, "What will I do now?" "How can I go on?"

I have never been one to sit still for long periods of time. So, being alone and grateful for the dawning of light, I decided to start the arduous process of taking care of business. The first thing was to make a list of what I thought needed to be done and who I needed to contact. You will find a similar checklist in the appendix. I realized there was plenty to do. On the one hand, I did not want to do anything but sit and think and cry. On the other hand, I was so miserable, I wanted to take my mind off of my situation. In retrospect, I understand the long-standing advice of not making any major decisions quickly. This is definitely *not* an old wives' tale. However lucid you may think you are, you are not that lucid! Had I gone with some of my initial reactions—moving, leaving my home, et cetera, I would have regretted it. Life and situations settle down, and you should just give it some time.

I do understand there are extenuating circumstances to counter this advice. Sometimes people need close family support for financial and health reasons. People may be afraid of being alone in a less-than-desirable neighborhood. But, as a general rule-of-thumb, avoid making any major decisions for at least a year, and for goodness sake, *do not* let your children or other family members pressure you into making decisions you may later regret.

On top of the normal business I had to take care of, there was a letter on my desk concerning our being audited by the Internal Revenue Service. John had filed our taxes for years. He always went over them with me, but I just let the information go in one ear and out the other. I trusted him, was not interested in the nitty-gritty of the finances, and, frankly, just did not want to be bothered. Even when I was single and had only the short form to complete, I hired an accountant. I had a mental block and a fear of dealing with taxes. Now, here I was faced with an audit and had no idea where to turn. I looked at all the tax notes and IRS jargon. I clasped my hands to my head and screamed. I might as well have been trying to decipher hieroglyphics!

I am convinced angels appear at the appropriate time. A couple of years before John's death, we changed stockbrokers. How this happened is a complete fluke. Our stockbroker(s) turned out to be a husband/wife team, and a friendship developed. They met with me numerous times to go over in great detail my finances and to help me plan for the future. It was through them I met an excellent and patient accountant. She took this financially-hysterical female and helped me sort through John's notes, old tax records, computer files, and other necessary documents. Unfortunately, the magic wand was not sufficient to keep me from paying Uncle Sam additional monies, but she saved my sanity and became a dear friend.

Let me backtrack. In August prior to John's death, my mother fell and broke her hip and leg. The damage was so extensive that she could not have a hip replacement, and there was no guarantee she would ever walk again. After surgery and recuperation in the hospital, she was moved to a nursing home for care and rehabilitation. She was in the nursing home when John died. As soon as Mother was to the point where she could receive physical therapy at home, my sister took her out of the nursing home. In November, Mother went to my sister's, but still needed a lot of care.

About three weeks after John died, I began sharing care time of Mother with my sister, Nancy Jo (I call her Nana). Nana lives about sixty miles from Mother's house. She would care for Mother a couple of weeks and then bring her home. I would make the 150-mile trip to Mother's and stay with her. This rotation of care and location continued until Mother's death. The following May, while at Nana's, Mother died suddenly of a heart attack. Mother's death meant additional estate business to take care of, but at least this time, it was shared with a sister and a brother. For me, this made dealing with Mother's estate business easier, but sometimes additional persons just complicate the process.

In June 1998, John and I began writing the biography of Alabama's former U.S. Senator Howell Heflin. Neither the research nor the writing was complete when John died. We also did not have a publisher for the book. I was determined that the book be completed and published as a tribute to John and to the Senator. As bittersweet as this project was, I persevered. In September 2001, NewSouth Books released *A Judge in the Senate: Howell Heflin's Career of Politics and Principle*. It was a slow, painful, and difficult process, but the book gave me a sense of pride, accomplishment, and a legacy for John.

Admittedly, all these activities—taking care of estate affairs, caring for Mother, completing the book, and ultimately, doing some consulting work—were an emotional and physical drain. Grief, alone, takes its own toll on a person's emotional and physical health. But, these activities also gave me a purpose, a reason to arise each morning, and helped me avoid going into the depths of depression.

So—here I went—one step forward and three back!

4

Where Have All the Casseroles Gone?

What do you do after all the relatives leave, the thank you notes are written, and the bills are paid? For the first few weeks, I was very occupied with these things. Sympathy cards arrived, notes and letters were received, friends and family members called and visited. I had invitations to lunch and dinner. And then—just as if a faucet were turned off—most of these activities ceased. There was an occasional card or note. A couple of my very special friends continued to call, visit, and invite me out, but for the most part, everyone went back to a normal routine, and I guess they thought I did, too. The trouble was, I no longer had a "normal" routine. My whole life had been upset.

Unless you have experienced it, you cannot realize the depth nor length of time grief takes. It is a slow, difficult process. Changes occur even in your own body system that you absolutely cannot control. Grief is my worst experience ever.

All of us are guilty of showing immediate reaction when some tragedy happens. We give of ourselves and our money. After the initial spurt, we soon fizzle out. What we do not realize is that it takes more than three or four weeks for the bereaved to heal.

A couple of weeks after John died, I was out eating breakfast with someone. I could barely force food into my system. I would literally choke. I ate a few bites and stopped. The other person looked at me, looked at my full plate of food, and exclaimed, "I am surprised at you. I thought you'd do better than this!" They were surprised that this person they knew as a tough, strong, take-charge individual had not yet gotten over John's death. Duh!?!

I will always be grateful for and indebted to a longtime friend who will be my example in what to do for others. She would not call and "ask" me if I needed anything or if I wanted to do something. Instead, she would call and say, "CR, I'm coming over and bringing some tea. We'll have a cup of hot tea together. If you want to talk, we will. If you just want to sit quietly, we will do that—whatever you want." Or, "I'm picking up sandwiches. It's a pretty day. We'll walk over to the park and eat." Or, "CR, there is an event at so-and-so. I'll pick you up and we'll go." These acts were lifesavers for me because it was hard to make any effort on my own

Nana's husband died of cancer a year before John. Nana and Barbara, John's sister, advised me not to cut myself off from social invitations, especially from couples. I made a concerted effort to do most of the things for which I was invited. Most invitations I accepted with dread and always with the temptation to cancel, but I found I could enjoy myself. Those outings took the focus away from my own misery and were positive for my mental health and healing. I also, deliberately, tried to go to places and do things that John and I did together. It was painful and difficult, but I figured the sooner I faced those challenges, the better I would be. I still believe I did the correct thing.

I found that the cards, notes, and calls that trickled in weeks and months later were precious. It was a learning experience for me. Even though you may not do something for someone immediately, it is never too late to express sympathy, send a 'thinking of you' card, make a phone call, or extend an invitation for an outing. These were so appreciated when the "let-down" occurred.

One thing in particular that shocked me was the world kept turning! I wrote in my journal,

> *Jesus! I just don't understand how the world is going on about its normal business when I am suffering so. Nobody seems to notice I am in such pain and agony. I want to scream out, "Stop! My husband and mother have died.*

I'm hurting! How can you be so nonchalant about this?" But they don't know, and the world keeps spinning. If I could just get off . . . What do I do?

After three or four weeks, I was basically on my own. The acts of sympathy became few and far between. As everyone else went along their merry way, I was grieving.

Mostly, I cried, moaned, and mourned in private. To others, I remained tough, strong, and smiling. Perhaps this is good to an extent. It forced me to be less self-focused. People get tired of hearing about your problems; most people have plenty of problems of their own. However, there were days I was so miserable inside and so happy on the exterior, I could have won an Oscar for my betrayal of "The Happy Widow."

I was also fortunate to have a good friend who is a trained minister/ counselor. His schedule was always available to allow me some time to talk and cry. His feedback and insights were invaluable in helping me to identify feelings that were valid, directions to take, and helped me keep focused

I will confess I turned down offers of group grief sessions in the beginning. There were several reasons for this: 1) I felt I was perfectly capable of handling my own grief; 2) I didn't want to "spill my guts" in front of strangers; and, 3) I didn't want to be faced with the possibility of a grieving male looking for a wife replacement (let's be honest here).

About fourteen months after John died, and about six months after Mother died, I did join a group grief session sponsored by my church. This six-week's program was facilitated by a church friend, and the small group that met weekly was made up of people I knew. I felt comfortable in this group, and we were all familiar with one another's losses. It was a time for sharing and reconfirmation of our love and support for each other.

Action Plan

What advice would I give to help you after the casseroles are eaten and you are left standing on the street alone?

1. Get out. Do not sit at home brooding. Yes, you need some time

alone, but resume as many of your former activities within the time frame in which you are comfortable. You do not have to start all at once—just take it one step at a time.

2. Avoid the tendency to "spill your guts" to everyone who comes along. Confide in a few close friends, family, or counselor, but otherwise, keep quiet. Most people are uncomfortable with others' tears and problems.

3. Talk about your deceased loved one. This is part of the healing process. Again, this does not mean being obsessive about it and talking about all the pain and agony over your loss. It does mean to talk normally about the deceased. Most people are already walking on "eggshells" around you, not knowing what to say or do. They are afraid that mentioning your loved one will make you uncomfortable, so talking openly and normally about your loved one will open the door for others.

4. Keep a sense of humor and keep things in perspective. You are not the first, the only one, nor will you be the last to experience this. It is okay to tell funny stories or jokes, in general, even about the deceased. Laughter is good medicine.

For those of you who are dealing with someone who has lost a loved one, here are some guidelines for you.

1. Be there. You do not have to SAY or DO anything. Just be there, if you can. Squeeze a hand. Give a hug. Say, "I'm sorry."

2. Relate a story. If you feel comfortable enough, relate some funny or meaningful story about the deceased. It will let the bereaved know that the deceased meant something special to you, too.

3. Listen. Spare some ear-time. Avoid giving advice or doing all the talking. Just let the bereaved talk, and you listen. Respond only when appropriate.

4. Send that card or note. Even if weeks have gone by and you feel embarrassed that you have not yet mailed the intended card, do so now. I found some of the sweetest moments came when an unexpected card or note arrived in the mail weeks and months

later. You do not have to purchase an expensive, factory-generated card. A simple note will suffice. I appreciate so much those who took the time to write me a personal note. Personal notes are an extra "I care" thought.

5. Remember that grief is lingering. Place a note on your calendar to do something at a later date. A pot of soup taken to the bereaved on the month anniversary of the death, an invitation to an outing three months later, a thinking-of-you card somewhere along the way, a phone call on the anniversary of the death or the birthday of the deceased—all these things are minute ways of saying, "I care." One special call came to me on Valentine's Day, just to see if I was okay and to tell me I was loved.

6. Hug. Some folks are huggers and some are not. Some folks like to be hugged and some do not. Use discretion with this. I am a hugger, but this only developed after years of being hugged by others. I am so comfortable with hugging, I forget that some people back off from this. But, as far as you and the bereaved are comfortable with it, hug. Physical touch (in a healthy manner) is needed.

7. Keep positive. Even though you may have your own set of problems, now is not the time to unload them on the bereaved. Find someone else in which to confide. Keep a positive and upbeat attitude around the bereaved.

It takes a village to deal with grief. Let us remember to share one another's burdens and to uplift each other. Let us not do this just in death but also in life.

5

Decisions, Decisions

Two of the major decisions I had to make were: Am I going to continue to live (physically)? If I continue to live, am I going to remain bogged down in grief?

For goodness sake, do not think these were one-time questions! I still have relapses when days are gloomy and things are not going well. I especially lapse into the "poor me" when I am tired, but these "pity" days are fewer and further between.

Especially in older couples, both spouses often die within a short time span. Prior to my own grief, I did not understand this. Now, I do. The sense of loss of one's spouse is overwhelming. There is a large void, not only in your physical day-to-day life, but inside your body. The heart actually aches; the heart is actually heavy. There is an overwhelming sense of aloneness. Grief took away my appetite. I felt horrible. I could have easily crawled into bed and stayed there, wasting away, and praying for death.

I will admit, I did not want to live. I had no desire to live. Furthermore, I could not see a reason for living. But, I had to face up to the reality that I had two choices: I could choose life, or I could choose death.

I thought seriously about my choices. In the end, I opted for life. For whatever reason(s), I concluded that I was meant to remain on this earth. At this point, I felt I did not have the right to take my own life—either by fast or slow methods. So, after lengthy discussions with myself and with God, I chose to live. To be brutally honest, it was not an easy decision. I think I finally got the message when I kept asking God to *let* me die, and He didn't comply!

I am sure others were worried about me. One day while in my physician's office, he asked, "Clara Ruth, do you ever entertain thoughts of suicide?" I truthfully answered that I did, but continued, "You don't have to worry about me. I wouldn't do that." (I was not too truthful at that point.) He replied, "Well, I hope not because that would make me very angry." I guess I did not actually want to commit suicide, but I did want to die. My physician told me that suicide is like a bird: there is no real harm if one flies overhead, but be careful that it doesn't nest in one's hair.

My second decision was whether or not to stay stuck in grief. My grief was overwhelming. I had lost my husband, my best friend, and my professional working partner all in one. I was faced with the possibility of long-term care for my mother. There seemed to be no positives in my life. I was emotionally, physically, mentally, and, yes, spiritually, depleted. I was consumed with grief. I felt enveloped by darkness.

About three months after John's death, I was driving the 150-miles from Mother's to my own home. I had cried most of the way. I was a basket case and should not have been on the road. Yes, I had been functioning—taking care of business, helping care for Mother, and going through the routine of daily living. I was not doing these things joyfully, gleefully, nor gratefully. It was by sheer willpower and the consciousness of putting one foot in front of the other. It was also prompted by the decision I made to live.

Well, back to my drive. Can you just imagine what other drivers must have thought? Here was this lady driving down the interstate, paper tissues strewn all over the car, a tissue in each hand holding onto the steering wheel, and sobbing almost uncontrollably. I am sure all the other drivers wanted to pass and get away from this crazy looking woman!

All of a sudden, a thought popped into my head. "Well, Missy (the term Mother used when she *really* meant for me to "straighten up"), you are facing a fork in the road. You can take this fork to your left and continue to wallow in your misery forevermore, or you can take this fork to the right, go through the NORMAL grief process, and have a life. What is it you *really* want?" Do not think I made this decision in a flash. It neither came quickly nor easily. It sounds funny to say, but as miserable as I was, there was some comfort in grief. I was justified! The grief gave me an excuse to collapse in on myself, to feel sorry for myself, to be self-focused, to have excuses, and, yes, by grieving, I felt I was "honoring" John's memory. If I chose the right fork, I would have to take responsibility. There would be no more of this "being a victim" stuff. Forget the self-pity. "So, where to, Missy?"

I eventually chose the right fork. I knew this was the harder of the two decisions. Mother needed me. I kept telling myself I could do this; I choose to do this; I choose to be strong.

How naïve I was in thinking that once I made this decision, everything would fall right into place!

6

Nothin' Worse Than a Cryin' Woman
(The Emotional Aspects of Grief)

The title of this chapter, "Nothin' Worse Than a Cryin' Woman," is a John expression. He, as most men, had a difficult time knowing how to react to women when they cried. He was completely bumfuzzled. Well, he would have been at a complete loss had he observed me after his death. Uncontrollable crying—that is the only way I know how to express it.

Before John's death, I was not much of a crier. I might get misty-eyed and a little teary at some mushy movie or book, but there were times when I felt blue or something happened, and I wished that I could cry. After John's death, the dam broke. All I could do was cry.

Mornings were the hardest for me. I would wake up retching and think, "How am I going to survive this day?" I would cry. Of course, I was surrounded by John's possessions. One glance at those would cause me to cry. Every time I had to mention John's death when taking care of business I would cry. I could pass someone on the street and they would say, "Hello," and I would cry. You get the picture.

All this crying was embarrassing as well as hard on my body. I always felt "drained," not relieved. My emotions had control over me; I did not have control over my emotions. The only positive was that the tissue companies were definitely making a profit. I am sure I used a couple of boxes of tissues a day.

I think the crying was my main expression of grief. When I discussed this excessive crying with my counselor/friend, he assured me that the crying was normal and that he would have been more concerned had I not cried. In reading some grief materials, it was noted that recent research reveals tears purge the body of the chemicals that build up in response to stress. I guess I had a lot to purge.

It is difficult to separate the physical, emotional, and mental aspects of grief. They are interconnected, and one affects the others.

The emotional side of grief certainly affected my physical state—the not eating, not sleeping, and the overwhelming fatigue. I was in a state of mourning, for sure. Though I had experienced deaths of other family members and close friends, none was as grievous as John's death. With others, I could mourn and then go on—my entire life was not affected. But, John's death touched every fiber of my being and every aspect of my daily life.

Mother's death caused a rebirth of all the grief symptoms from which I thought I was beginning to recover. Mother was 84 years old and had lived a good life. She was tired, and her eight-month's recuperation process wearied her even more. She was adamant about not being a burden on her children. In all areas, she was ready to leave the world. It is hard to let go of a parent, but at the same time, you always expect them to die before you.

I was thankful Mother's death came swiftly and she did not have to spend years in a nursing home. I am thankful she did not have years of suffering and pain. She died with her mental acuity. I mouned more for me. I had no "parental home"—the house was there, but it was Mother that made it home.

Though I felt I was grieving for Mother, Daddy, and John all at the same time, I am not so sure because I was so caught up in my grief for John. My grief was so deep, there were times I did not know whom or what I *was* grieving for. It was like being in a pot of stew—all mixed up and not being able to identify one part from another.

If a fortune-teller had told me that at this time in my life I would be a widow and an orphan, I would never have believed it. It is true we never know what events—perhaps life changing events—a day can bring. We hear it over and over, that life is short and we need to make the most of each day. I now know the truth of that statement. Life is tenuous. It can be snapped from us in a single breath. My personal experiences are testimony to this.

The realities of life are hard. As the psalmist says, we walk *through* the valley of death. The deceased walks on through that valley to the other side. It takes the bereaved a lot longer to get through that valley. We have to linger, wander around a while, and get lost a few times to make it through. Little by little, we catch a glimpse of the sunshine, and eventually we walk out of that valley. The memories of those shadows are not so easily left behind. Memories remain, pain remains, but little by little, a new life—hopefully a changed but happy life—will emerge.

Action Plan

After a loved one dies, how do we maintain our emotional health?

1. If you feel like crying, do so. After several weeks, try, if possible, to control your public crying. Unfortunately, our society feels like John did; they are very uncomfortable with another's tears.

2. If you continue to be blue and to cry constantly, see your doctor. There are non-habit forming medications to help you if your "normal" grief becomes depression.

3. Join a grief support group. There you will find others who have experienced or are experiencing what you are going through. They can help you and give you guidance and direction.

4. Take control. The longer you let someone else do for you, the longer you will remain in grief. Though others are well-meaning, you are the one who will eventually have to go it alone. The sooner you can get in charge, the better.

5. Remember, bad days will continue for months and maybe years. Allow yourself some "down" time, but then get up and get going again.

6. Stay busy. Sitting and dwelling on your situation is not healthy and is not going to change anything. Do something!

7. Think of others. Avoid being so self-centered. When you feel blue, think of someone else who needs help and do something for

him/her. Do not expect someone to always come to your aid; go to someone else's aid.

8. Do something nice for yourself. Pamper yourself. Take care of yourself. This can be as simple as a day in the beauty shop, a round of golf with special friends, a morning in bed with the paper and coffee, or a sinful ice cream cone.

9. Nurture your spiritual life.

10. Avoid making a shrine of your deceased and his/her personal items. It is okay to rearrange the furniture, move photos, and make your surroundings comfortable for you.

There are also ways that you can help another who is grieving.

1. Be there. Bring a box of tissues, and do not be intimidated by another's tears.

2. Listen. Let the grieved one talk, not you.

3. Motivate the bereaved to get out and to get on with life, but do not ignore the fact that the bereaved needs sufficient mourning time.

4. Avoid making the bereaved into an "invalid." You may help, but avoid doing everything for them.

Following are some action thoughts to take *before* a loved one dies:

1. Make the most of every day. Though this may sound trite, it is certainly worth putting into practice. To use an overused term, "Take time to smell the roses."

2. Do it NOW! This does not mean going in debt to get everything materially you want. It could mean, however, to start saving for that special vacation or whatever. Stop procrastinating and invite those friends over to dinner. The meal does not have to be perfect; the house does not have to be finely decorated or spotless. Leave the housework and play with the children or grandchildren. Whatever it is that you have wanted to do, take that first step TODAY!

3. Remember that grief is a natural process—as natural as being

born and dying—but we neither think about it nor are we prepared for it when it happens. Learn about grief through activities such as reading this book so that you will not be so surprised when all this happens to you. It will also make you more supportive and understanding of others who are experiencing grief.

4. Determine your priorities. Sit down and decide what it is you really want to do and be. What is most important in your life? Once you have determined it, act on it. If your spouse is the most important, stop ignoring him/her. Give your spouse your best.

5. Let people know you love them and appreciate them.

6. Laugh and maintain a sense of humor. I cannot emphasize this enough.

7. Know when to fight, and choose your battles wisely. In retrospect, most battles are not worth the energy. Before you get into a fuss with a loved one, stop, count to ten, and ask yourself, "What does this matter in the long run, in the whole scheme of things?" Most of the time, it is pride that gets us into battles.

8. Control your anger. Breathe deeply and relax. Too many hurtful words are said in anger. Do not end the day on an angry note.

9. As much as possible, avoid regrets. Ask yourself, "If I (or my loved one) died today, what regrets would I have?" Do not be left with regret over things left undone or unsaid. Try to amend the regrets, starting *now*. Try your best to avoid any future regrets.

All the above are things we already know. We just need to be reminded of them and to make them a part of our daily lives.

7

Do I Look Bad or What?
(The Physical Aspects of Grief)

Grief is not just a matter of the "heart"; grief takes a physical toll on the body. I would loosely compare grief to surgery. In surgery, one is put to sleep, some diseased part is removed, and the patient is carefully monitored and cared for until health returns. In grief, the sensation is more like having your favorite body part ripped away under protestation without anesthesia. No stitches or bandages cover the wound; it is exposed for all to see. The pain is raw, intense, throbbing, and ever present. There are no painkillers to dull the ache. It takes very little for the wound to become inflamed all over again. However, in both cases, time is important in the healing process; the healing cannot be rushed.

As I mentioned earlier, I had no appetite, no hunger pangs. Having a foods and nutrition background, I knew I had to eat in order to maintain my own health. Solid food was almost impossible for me to swallow. I would choke. I was under such stress, my throat muscles were constricted. I could drink liquids, so I purchased instant breakfast powder and milk and that became my sustenance. For added nutrients and calories, I often mixed in some yogurt or ice cream. Even after I returned to eating solid foods, I could not eat much, so I supplemented my diet with the liquid mixture.

People were generous in sending me grief material. In one source, I read that approximately 85 percent of people who lose a spouse have a serious illness within one year of the death. I can certainly understand that statistic, but I was determined not to be one. I consciously made the decision to keep my body as fit and as healthy as I could.

Not being able to eat was only one aspect of the food problem. I was also eating alone. John and I almost always shared our mealtime. So even eating was a huge reminder of my loss. Even now, I read or watch television when I am dining alone, and there are still times I have to force myself to eat.

Food is also a reminder of our social life. John and I loved to entertain, and we often had guests. I would most likely cook rather than our eating out. When I resumed entertaining, it was difficult seeing John's empty chair and having no host to help me.

I lost too much weight. In a conversation with friends, I commented, "When I was little . . ." One of my friends laughed and said, "Clara Ruth, you have always been little." That is true, though my weight has varied over the years, mostly due to my exercise program or lack of it. So, I had little extra weight to lose. When eating resumed, my weight returned.

Cooking for one is no fun. Some people will cook for themselves. Mother did. She never went a day, when her health permitted, that she did not cook a full meal. Not I. So I ate—and still do—lots of fruits, salads, cottage cheese, cheese, yogurts, nutritional shakes, nuts, peanut butter, and other non-cook items. I will sometimes cook a pot of soup and freeze portions that can be popped into the microwave at a later date. I like to bake, so I will bake nutritionally-packed breads and freeze them to use when I want. I try to stay away from the snack foods such as chips, cookies, and such. I know the foods that I do eat must be nourishing.

Fatigue! Fatigue! Fatigue! It takes a lot of energy to go through the grief process. For a while, it was all I could deal with. It was a chore to get up out of bed or to do anything. I was tired to the bone, but even then I could not sleep. I know this sounds contradictory—just like a lot of other statements involving grief. I was so fatigued all I wanted to do was lie in bed. When I was lying there, sleep did not come and all the thoughts were focused on "poor me." To counter this, I stayed busy. I gave in to the depths of grief at times, but I forced myself not to stay there.

Only twice have I had dreams about John. I understand dreaming about the deceased is normal. I just do not fit the "normal" pattern, I guess. Both dreams I had were ones in which John appeared to me, but told me he could not stay. In one of the dreams, after telling me he was here only temporarily, he asked, "Does Gorman [our physician] know I'm dead?" I thought, "Why silly, of course he does. He is the one who pronounced you dead." It is amazing the workings of the brain.

Gradually, my normal sleep pattern returned. One day while in my physician's office for one of my frequent check-ups (man, did he keep close tabs on me), he asked how I was doing. I answered that I was okay. He looked me in the eye, accused me of not being truthful and said, "You look absolutely awful." At the time, I did not see it. In retrospect and hearing comments from friends and family, who were all much too nice at the time to tell me, I did look pretty awful. Imagine, if you can, this pale, dark-circled-hollow-eyed, skinny person walking around with a tear drenched tissue in her hand. Pathetic!

Finally, my physician convinced me I needed help with sleeping. I had to let go of my pride, which had convinced me I could overcome this all "by myself." My body had a new sleep routine—a bad one. He gave me a non-habit forming, mild, anti-depressant useful for sleeping. I found that a half a tablet was all I needed at first, then I cut back to a fourth. After about three months, I did not need the medication. My body had adjusted to a new sleep routine. Normal sleep returned. Occasionally, when I have difficulty sleeping, I will take the medication for a few nights. That is all I need to resume a normal sleep pattern.

I also exercised to overcome the fatigue, which sounds contradictory. My personal experience and training had taught me that physical exercise is necessary for good health. Since I was making a conscious effort to preserve my health, I knew—tired or not—I had to exercise. I did some stretching exercises and calisthenics. I walked 30 minutes five days a week. Later, I alternated between walking and riding an exercise bike. The exercise was a great stress reliever. The exercise regime made such a positive difference in the way I felt and in my mental outlook, it has become a habitual part of my life. Using weights a couple of times a week rounds out my exercise program. I am probably healthier and more fit now than I have been in years.

As I have previously mentioned, I am not much of a "group" person. I am self-motivated, so am perfectly content to do my exercise program alone. For those who need outside motivation and support, join a gym or a walking group. Get an exercise buddy. Just EXERCISE!

Action Plan

You do not have to succumb to being a "walking wounded." Baring other, underlying physical problems, you can stay physically healthy. You owe it to yourself and to your family to remain as healthy as you possibly can. There are some hints to help you do this.

1. Eat right. You do not have to be a cook to have a healthy diet. Stock your refrigerator and pantry with low-sodium/low-fat soups that can be heated in the microwave; fresh fruits; vegetables, such as carrots, celery, broccoli, prepackaged salads and cole slaw; canned fruits (packed in its own juice or water) and fruit juice; yogurt, cottage cheese, reduced-fat cheeses and milk; instant breakfast powder; instant oatmeal and cold cereal; peanut butter; whole wheat bread and crackers; and nuts. Eggs, in moderation, are an excellent source of protein and can easily be prepared by boiling or by breaking into a microwavable dish and zapping them for several seconds. Use deli meats in moderation because they can be high in sodium and fat. Dry roasted peanuts, soy nuts, and low-fat popcorn are also good additions to the diet. Avoid caffeine as much as possible. Also avoid the high sugar, high fat products, especially chips, cookies, candy, and such. They provide little nutritional value. When the appetite is diminished, you need to pack a "nutritional punch" with the foods you do consume.

2. Exercise. This one is tough, but just DO IT. It is easy to lie in bed or sit on the sofa, stare into space, and put it off until "tomorrow." The road of a thousand miles begins with the first step. Walk.

Walk up and down the stairs, around the outside of your house, in a park, in a mall, around the neighborhood. Bike, using either a regular or a stationary bike. Golf. Play tennis. Swim. Dance. Join a gym. Just do SOMETHING and do it on a regular basis.

3. Sleep. Your body really needs more sleep than usual to help you heal from the stress. If you feel like napping, do so. Give in to the desire for sleep. If you are having difficulty sleeping, do not be too proud to ask your physician for some temporary help with this problem.

4. Maintain a good relationship with your physician. Get a good physical, and follow your physician's advice. Be honest and open with your physician as to any problems you might be having.

5. Remember, time does help the healing process, but you must do your part!

8

Do I Be Crazee?
(The Mental Aspects of Grief)

Honestly, I thought I was losing my mind. Had it not been for my sister who confessed to the same experience after her husband died, I would have been greatly worried. I *was* worried anyway because I was not sure mine, at least, was not permanent.

What prompted these feelings of insanity? For one thing, it was difficult for me to concentrate. I would read a section of the newspaper or a book, and then realize I had no earthly idea what I had read. I would just sit and stare at the written word.

Television held no attraction for me. I could not even sit long enough to watch the evening news. I still have difficulty watching television. Part of it may be that there is little on television worth my time, and part may be that I never watched television alone. Television was an activity John and I shared.

Another example is that I would start to tell something and absolutely lose my train of thought in mid-sentence. My mind would blank out. I could not remember what I was saying or where I was going with the story. It was exasperating, annoying, and embarrassing.

Losing items or papers seemed to become the norm for me. Always described as an organized, detailed, and "knowing where things are" person—as long as I was the one who placed them there—I became completely hopeless. This was very disturbing. I was perplexed when some items turned up in very obscure places.

These "symptoms" turned into a Catch 22 situation: the more I experienced these things, the more stress it caused. In turn, the more stress I was under, the more I experienced the lack of concentration.

The lack of concentration was not my only problem. I went through a time when I had no desire to do much of anything that required mental acuity. However, I was forced to use my mental ability in taking care of estate business, a tax audit, and such. After about three months, I resumed work on the biography when my level of concentration started improving. I really had to work hard to keep focused.

Though I was sure it would not be long before I would be institutionalized or was definitely developing early onset of dementia, being reminded that this was a normal reaction of grief eased my fears. I had once read that if you are aware you cannot remember, then you do not have dementia. It is only when you are not aware you cannot remember that there is cause for alarm.

Even after the initial fog lifted from my brain, I experienced relapses from time to time, especially when fatigued or stressed. At least I had a legitimate excuse!

Once I was visiting friends, and we were traveling in the car. I was in the middle of some story and stopped. I had no idea what I was telling or why. My friend turned around and looked at me sitting in the back seat, grinned, and remarked, "Having a senior moment, are we?"

Whatever the task, it was several months before my concentration returned to normal. Thankfully, I feel more in control of my senses, and am grateful I can sit and read the newspaper, a book, or carry on conversations without drifting into a fog pond.

Action Plan

There are some ways to help yourself through this mental fogginess.

1. Keep the brain as active as possible during this time even though you may not feel like it.
2. Avoid making major decisions while you are in this state. It is recommended to wait at least a year on important decisions.
3. Know that a decline in mental acuity is normal for a period of

time. No two people experience the exact grief symptoms for the same amount of time. So, do not fret.

4. As much as is possible, avoid stress and stressful situations. Stress just makes the matters worse.

5. Get plenty of rest and sleep. Even under normal conditions, the brain becomes dull and foggy when one is tired and sleep deprived. With grief, it is exaggerated.

6. Write the memoirs of your loved one. It is amazing how quickly you forget a lot of things when that person is not there to remind you of them. Make a memory book. It not only will give you something to do, but will be a nice way to pass along those memories to other family members.

There are also some ways for you to help others who are grieving:

1. Offer support and keep reinforcing the fact that this mental confusion will pass.

2. Avoid pushing the bereaved into making any major decisions for a while. Allow them time to adjust to their new situation and give them time to think.

3. Be patient with the lapses of memory. Avoid chiding or fussing.

4. Offer help in locating lost items. But remember, there is a fine line between being bossy and being patronizing.

5. Help the bereaved to stay busy. Urge them to stay active. Physical activity helps keep the mind active.

9

Has God Forsaken Me?
(The Spiritual Aspects of Grief)

My faith was visibly shaken after John's death. It was a contradictory mix of feelings. When John was suffering so terribly toward the end, I fervently prayed for God to heal him or to have mercy on him. It was too painful for me to watch John struggling for breath. Hoping against hope that something could be done to restore John to health proved futile. So, when John died, I felt no anger toward John or God. Many people have expressed to me their anger against both God and their loved one when the loved one died.

The "Why Me?" question was not and is not part of my vocabulary either. Whether this is due to knowing my grandmother, mother, mother-in-law, sister, and friends lost a spouse, I do not know. However painful, I know death touches all persons, and I knew I had not been singled out to be "zapped." As badly as I hurt, I would never wish that same hurt on someone else.

As time evolved, my questioning began. I reverted to those questions I had prior to John's death, in addition to new ones that kept popping up. John sometimes accused me of being a cynic—and he would have really pointed his finger at me during this time. I have always felt that faith is meaningless if you just accept someone else's interpretation without questions, study, thought, and, yes, even doubt.

My questions ranged from "With all the complicated diseases we have cures and effective medicines for, why was John taken because of asthma?" "John was such a contributor to this world, why was he taken and some poor comatose soul in a nursing home or some wife abuser remain?" "John loved life and wanted to live. Were he and I being punished in some way?" John and I had a very close relationship. "Why was he taken when there are so many couples who couldn't care less if their spouse died? Why was Mother taken when I was already so mired in grief?"

Then, there were other questions. "Why is this grief so over-whelming? Why can I not get over this pain?" "Why does God give us someone to love so deeply and then yank them away from us and make us suffer so deeply for so long?" It was suggested that I read "Biblical words of comfort" about sorrow, grief, and joy. Frankly, these words were hollow to me.

Oh, my list could go on and on. I have never doubted the existence of God, but I certainly doubted His love and concern for me. A whole bag of "theological worms" were opened, and I am still dealing with a lot of these issues. Not all of these issues were a result of grief—they just became more exposed when my soul was torn open.

Some of the issues I have resolved. With others, I am still in a wrestling match. Just as with the rest of me, I am in a spiritually evolutionary process. I have discovered some of the things I had been told as a child—and with which I grew up—are just not true. But, I have found these issues have been replaced with stronger and more loving truths.

In our last conversation, when John knew he was dying, he told me to be sure to count my blessings instead of my sorrows. Though hard to fathom, it was good advice. God is still the same in the bad times as He is in the good times. When things are going badly, it is hard to remember to count blessings, to focus on the positives, and to keep trudging onward.

Action Plan

How can we remain spiritually strong during and after this time of grief?

1. Remember, it is okay to be angry with God (and the deceased).

Scream! Yell! Question! Express that anger. It is natural. But again, if you find you cannot let go of that anger after a reasonable period of time, seek help either from a trained counselor or a member of the clergy. The same goes for guilt.

2. Question. If your faith is worth anything at all, it can withstand your doubts and questions. It might be helpful to discuss these doubts and questions with spiritually strong, but open-minded and loving people. I happen to have very strong, loving, and understanding family and friends who helped me.

3. Work through it. Do not just throw out your faith. Talk to your clergy, being open in all your thoughts.

4. Get involved in a church, synagogue, or other house of worship. Surround yourself with faith-centered people.

5. Pray. Ask God daily for strength and understanding. If you find you cannot pray, do as my minister suggests: rely on the prayers of others, enlisting others to be your words while you just take care of the sighs, groans, or silence.

6. Do not be afraid of change. Letting go of some of the old ideas and beliefs may allow you to be more loving, understanding, and compassionate, and less judgmental and biased.

7. Remember that the God who is with you in good times is also the God who is with you in bad times.

8. Remember, too, that even in a bad situation you can find some good, such as the love and support of family, friends, and the ordinary folks who make our lives more comfortable.

9. Keep a sense of humor. You will never know the answers to most of your questions, so look for the humor in life.

10. Remember, you can either throw out your faith completely or you can work through the issues of anger, hurt, pain, disappointment, and guilt. The choice is yours.

The most important advice I can give to anyone dealing with the grief-stricken is *NOT* to say that this happened for the best. Also, refrain from "preaching" and chiding if spiritual doubts arise. Let the bereaved work through these issues on his/her own terms, own time, and with your support.

As Karen Katafiasz says in her book, *Finding Your Way through Grief,* (1995), "You may rage at God for permitting this loss. You may doubt God's goodness. You may feel as if God betrayed you—you who strove to live rightly, who prayed devotedly, who assumed that God would protect you. You may abandon God as indifferent, distant, useless, or even non-existent. Let yourself rail and raise your fist in fury; let yourself walk away if you must. But don't conclude that this new arid place in which you find yourself is the final stop."

10

Eek! A Widow!
(The Social Aspects of Grief)

A divorcee—ooh la la! A widow—eek! Run for your life!

There may/will come a time after the death of your spouse when you wish to get into the social scene through dating. Thoughts of marriage may be dancing in your head. Now what? This can be an awfully scary time.

Well, first of all, let me tell you I am no expert in this area. I can only relate to you my experiences and pass along tips from others.

Right after John died, I vehemently declared I would never remarry. I was a "one man woman." Even the thoughts of another man in my life—so called "taking John's place"—nauseated me. People would say to me, "You are young and attractive, you will find someone else." I would reply, rather briskly, "Not me. I've had my husband!"

When John was in the hospital for the last time, lying there, he patted the side of the bed and said, "Come sit here; we need to talk." Instinctively, I knew what he was going to tell me, and I started crying. He said, "Now, we can't talk if you are going to do *THAT*!" (Remember, I told you John's feelings about crying women.) I wiped my tears but kept letting out verbal gulps during the ensuing conversation.

It was then John informed me he was not going "to make it." When I protested, he continued to tell me that "yes" he was going to die; "this time things are different." My only regret is that I was so distraught I could only talk about what to do and a little bit about our life together. I could not bring myself to discuss his dying process. This was our last discussion; he was no longer able to say much. Then he proceeded to give me instructions on what to do.

Tears involuntarily streamed down my face. Among the instructions given to me by John was to remarry after a couple of years. I protested again. He continued with the same verbiage I have heard since he died, about my being too young to stay single, I had too much to offer someone, and I needed companionship. I certainly thought he had already entered the twilight zone!

Several months passed. I suppose I was still in the shock stage of grief. I was also too busy caring for Mother, dealing with estate matters, and hell-bent on getting our book completed and published.

Then, it seemed one day I was overcome with this sense of being alone. Right now, I am not really sure what happened. Probably Mother's death caused me to rethink matters. I found myself with no one to accompany me to the symphony, no one to serve as host when I entertained friends, no companion when eating out, and no daily conversation.

With Mother's death, my cord of connectiveness was cut. Even though I have a brother and a sister, each has their own family. I felt like a cork floating out in the middle of the ocean.

I had no one beside me in bed, no ironing of shirts (well—truthfully I did not miss the extra ironing). I had none of those things I had been used to for almost twenty-four years. That ache, heaviness, and void in my "heart" grew larger and larger. I became more depressed and wished I could die—but not before the book was published, mind you! I desperately wanted someone to fill John's place.

Now, this is where the red flag goes up. Do *not* fall into this trap. At this stage in grief, you are very vulnerable. I have known some folks—men and women—who have married very quickly after the death of their spouse (and I will use one year or less as quickly). Some have had successful marriages and others have awakened one morning thinking, "Uh-oh—what have I done?" Remember that grief has to run its course, and you cannot just *replace* your lost loved one.

Our society is conditioned these days with the "Replacement Theory."

That is, if it breaks, replace it. This includes pets and spouses. Even a friend of mine who lost her baby a couple of months into her pregnancy was obsessed with getting pregnant again. She admitted she was intent on replacing that loss. That void creates such a barren waste that the natural instinct is to fill it.

Now, I am no smarter than the rest of you, but I recognized how vulnerable I was. So, I can easily see why some people marry soon after their spouse dies.

With all the changes in your life after the death of a spouse, one unexpected change, for me at least, was my relationship with the opposite sex. All of a sudden I was no longer in the "safe zone." I had to be careful I did not invoke jealousy in a wife. After all, "young widows" could be competition! Hugging the opposite sex has to be done carefully, and words have to be thought about before being spoken. Now, I have to make sure I am not perceived as flirting!

To paraphrase Popeye, "I yam what I yam." I have been described as being perky and friendly. Even in my young and single years this was often mistaken for flirting. Now, I have to be extra careful that my demeanor is not misconstrued.

And, as a widow you have to understand that some men perceive you as being "needy," and to be blunt, that means sexually needy. Naturally, they think they are the remedy. I have had a couple of these incidences but one, in particular, was very hurtful. A long-time friend made very improper advances toward me. Instead of being angry at him, my first thought was, "What image am I portraying? What does he think I am?" Then, I realized that he knows who I am. Many years of friendship had defined that.

Then I got very angry at him and very hurt. Why did he do this? Why did he betray John's and my friendship with him? How could he? Then I got angry at God. I was standing in my dining room, screaming out (literally) to God and crying. "Why? Haven't I been through enough without *this*? Why didn't you protect me from this? Why? Why?" (This is another question on my list for God.)

I must tell you that the dining room is close to the front door. I happen to have a mail slot in the front door. Lo and behold, while I am in the middle of this screaming tirade, in plops the mail! I know the mailman heard all my goings-on and was probably frightened by this madwoman's ranting and raging. I purposefully kept my distance from him from then on; we have since gotten a new mailman.

If you think these unwelcome advances will not apply to you, do not be so sure of yourself. They have also happened to friends of mine of both sexes, who were also unprepared for such advances.

WARNING! Be careful. Be yourself, but be prudent in your behavior.

I got over the vulnerable hurdle, or at least I felt I did. I realized that as badly as I wanted male companionship, I was not ready for it. I was not ready to accept another male for who he was. It would have been to fill John's place. This would not have been a fair proposition for a potential candidate. And, I discovered that dating left me angry. Why did I have to go through this? I did not want to date! Yes, I did want companionship, but I just did not want to be a part of the dating game.

Back to "eek." One thing I have discovered, with most single men, is that as soon as they find out I am a widow, they seem to get very quiet (almost reverent) and pull back. I might as well say, "Hello, my name is Clara Ruth, and I have leprosy." I doubt they would react any differently. Does the image of a widow denote "holiness," being untouchable, or being confined to a glass case? Or does the term conjure up that image of "black widow"—referring, of course, to a black widow spider that pounces on its prey and kills it? Perhaps the term automatically connects with marriage, from which a lot of men run. Does it infuse a feeling of sympathy or sadness? I am not sure of the answer, but if you are skeptical, just notice people's reactions when you tell them you are a widow. Somehow, I think "widower" is different—and means "eligible."

Let us now look at the scenario of a divorcee. Wow! Ears pick up, eyes twinkle, and there are thoughts of "fun and games." I have a widower friend who met a 60-year old divorcee. He called me with a lilt in his voice, "CR, do you think I can handle a divorcee?" Now, let us be honest. Do you think he would have called and asked the same question if the woman was a widow? Of course not!

Divorcee—fun, exotic, lively, sexy, interesting, red-hot.

Widow—dull, dark, sad, lonely, old, somber, holy, hands-off, married.

I cannot relate any personal experiences regarding remarriage. In talking with others, they have told me that an ache always remains for the deceased. You cannot forget or ignore the person who was intimately involved in your life. There will always be a spot reserved for the deceased, and if you have children, they are reminders of your deceased spouse. However, life does and can go on. Many told me that their second marriage is as loving and fulfilling as the first one. It is just different, but then again, they married a different person. This feeling does not cast a shadow on the deceased, but perhaps it is a compliment. More than one soulmate is possible.

Well, what about me? Do I think there will ever be a new soulmate for me? There are still unanswered questions. Frankly, I think I prefer not to live the remainder of my years alone. I love to travel, go to events, and to entertain. I prefer to have a partner in these activities. I love having a partner across from me at the breakfast and dinner table every day—full of lively discussion. Without sounding arrogant, I do not want just anyone, however. I want someone as special to me—in his own way—as John was to me in his own way, but certainly he must have a sense of humor.

Now, if we can just conjure up a replacement word for *widow* that shows there is still life in the ole gal yet…

Action Plan

So, what advice do I give you, being the novice I am in this category?

1. First, BEWARE! Do not rush into any relationship regardless of how lonely or alone you feel. Avoid being vulnerable. Some people have lost everything they own by others playing on their weakness.

2. Do not discount singles who have been long-time friends. You already have a history with them, and they may prove to be your

most enduring relationship.

3. If you have children, consider the impact of a new marriage on them and on their inheritance. Have everything understood with the children and the new mate, and be sure to put it in writing.

4. Do not compromise your values/principles to alleviate your loneliness. You can have a happy life with another person. You can have a fulfilling life alone.

II

Oh, the Holidays!

I suppose when Christians think of holidays, the first thought is Christmas. For any grieving person, the holidays include birthdays, anniversaries, family reunions and other gatherings, as well as the usual holidays. Any of these occasions can be a very painful time because they are all enveloped with memories. Sometimes these memories are of sadder times, but usually the memories revolve around happier moments. Now you have to face these special days without your loved one. A gloom has settled over these once-happy occasions.

John died in October. It seemed the holidays came in rapid succession—Halloween, Veteran's Day, my birthday, Thanksgiving, his birthday, Christmas, New Year's, and Valentine's. That first New Year's Eve without John was extremely painful because it was the eve of the millennium. John was so excited about seeing 2000 come into fruition. There was so much hype about the "new century" and all the dire predictions. John thought this was very humorous and could not wait to see what would happen. Of course, he never made it, and it was Mother and me facing the new year together.

All these special occasions are difficult. When everyone else is happy and having a wonderful time, you are sad and depressed. Most people feel that holidays are a time for family. There are many expectations. And, here you are with a big gaping hole in your heart. It is compounded by the fact that you are putting on a happy face.

Guilt often surrounds the holidays, too. Guilt for what you did to the deceased you should not have done or that special gift he/she really wanted and you were too cheap to purchase, or here you are finding moments of fun and enjoyment when you should be mourning. The list expands. Guilt and resentment are also associated with the fact that you do not want to decorate or do those usual things, but you feel like you should.

I was at Mother's during Thanksgiving after John's death. She asked, "Are we going to put up a Christmas tree this year?" My heart certainly said "no." The last thing I wanted to do was to decorate a tree, put a wreath on the door, and prepare a Christmas dinner. However, I kept my thoughts to myself and did all the above. In retrospect, I am so happy I put my own feelings aside and did it. It turned out to be Mother's last Christmas. Somehow, I survived all the first year holidays, and now have a more realistic view of what I can and cannot do.

It is amazing how little things can knock you for a loop. The first Christmas, I knew I needed to do some shopping—or at least I thought I needed to do some shopping. So, I psyched myself up. I did okay in a couple of stores. Then I went into the local K-Mart. As I walked in, the first thing I saw was a cooler full of eggnog. I lost it right there in the store and started sobbing uncontrollably. I just could not continue—seeing the eggnog hit me full force that John was dead. He looked forward to Christmas just for the eggnog!

The third Christmas I was on the booksigning tour with the Howell Heflin biography. It seemed that every bookstore and mall were playing Christmas music. The booksignings were already a very emotional experience for me—reminders that John, who should have been there, was not. Now, here was the Christmas music blaring, telling me to be happy and joyful. Bah! Humbug! I thought, "If I hear 'I'll Be Home for Christmas' one more time, I will literally throw up my hands and leave!" The booksignings in combination with the holiday activities, decorations, and music plummeted me into another bout of grief. Consequently, I ignored most of Christmas and its festivities.

Action Plan

For those facing special occasions and holidays without their loved one, I will give the following advice:

1. Plan ahead. Decide what you want to do and what you feel comfortable in doing for each special occasion. By planning, there will be fewer opportunities where surprises will send you into grieving.

2. Decide what parts of tradition you want to keep and what parts you want to discard. It is okay to make changes. Avoid inflicting guilt on yourself or letting others inflict guilt upon you when you make these changes. Even if you keep the same traditions, just remember that the circumstances have changed, so nothing will ever be just as it was.

3. Accept your limitations. Just do what you can do in terms of baking, shopping, entertaining, socializing, and such.

4. Take care of yourself by getting sufficient exercise, rest, and eating nutritious foods.

5. Remember that it is okay to feel sad. Sometimes, you may feel sad and happy all at the same time.

6. Confide in someone or attend a holiday grief seminar. Expressing your feelings openly is healthy.

7. Also remember that holidays and special occasions are opportunities for focusing on and doing for others. However, do not forget to be good to yourself.

For those dealing with a grieving person during holidays or special occasions, do not forget them. Make a special effort to make them feel loved and supported. Respect their feelings about how to celebrate the occasion, and do not force them into doing something that makes them feel uncomfortable.

12

What Now?

As I write this chapter, I am wondering just as you probably are—what now? My life has been forever changed. My days and my routines are different. I can cook when I want, stay up as late as I want, and let the laundry pile up. In other words, I make my own schedule.

My social life is different. I attend fewer events. I entertain less. The majority of my friends are couples, and I no longer fit in as comfortably as I once did in all the activities. I do not go out to eat on a whim because it now involves calling around to find someone who is available to go with me. I confess, I am not a comfortable "go-out-alone" person.

I am more serious-minded. Life has slapped me across the face and definitely gotten my attention. I do not have that daily stimulation of in-depth discussion as I had with John. Even though I continue to read and be involved, I am more introspective. I realize how short life really is. I see how people are wasting their time on battles that are not worth fighting. I am distraught at broken marriages and couples that do not make the most of their time together.

I see the realities of life. No matter how good life is, I see the sorrow most people will face—caring for elderly parents, loss of family members, illness. It is good we do not have a crystal ball to tell our future.

As with most widows, my financial status has changed. So, I budget carefully and wisely as I am the only person responsible for me.

Action Plan

So where do *I* go from here? Where do *you* go from here? What do *we* need to do?

1. Accept yourself—who you are, what you are, and who you are to become.

2. Keep the faith and believe in yourself and in your abilities. Life goes on. The world keep on turning no matter how much you want it to stop or to turn back the time. Even though things seem dark and hopeless, it is important to remember that the sun will shine again. The events I have encountered are no different from the millions that have gone before me. The difference is that I am experiencing them. Whatever explanation you choose to explain these happenings, each of us will face difficult circumstances and events in our life. But, we must continue to keep our focus on the positive.

3. Get involved. It would be very easy for me to become a loner, to sit and concentrate on my problems and myself. After all, that is my primary focus these days. It is a ME world instead of an US world. When I feel I am getting too self-focused, I have to give myself a talk and do something. I call a friend and go to lunch, volunteer at one of my organizations, make cookies to give away, write a card. I just have to remember to stay involved in life— physically, mentally, emotionally, socially, and spiritually.

4. Think positively. Negative thoughts bring negative results. Positive thoughts bring better things to your life in the form of better health, interesting friends, and happier circumstances. When bad moods and bad thoughts creep into your mind, consciously replace them with good thoughts, smiles, and positive words. When I keep myself smiling and I think positive thoughts, I feel better physically, emotionally, and mentally. Also, remember people get tired of being around someone who is mournful, sad, complaining, and negative. Empty your mind of the bad. Visualize replacing the bad with good and positive things. Negative

thoughts and actions cannot reside in the same space as positive ones.

5. Count your blessings. When you see how many good things you have left, it will help you face the future. With the losses I sustained in John's and my parents' deaths, there have been many good things added to my life. I have seen what wonderful family and friends I really do have, I have made new friends, I have gotten involved in new activities, and I know I can still be strong!

6. Use your pain and grief for good. Help someone else through his/her pain and grief. You can do more than sympathize. You can *empathize!* I cannot explain physical death or grief. However, I have to look for ways to transform this hurt, pain, and evil to something good. As remote as that seems, it can and does happen. I can now reach out to others in a way I could not before. I am cognizant of the preciousness of life. I know the value of family and friends and so I make a special effort to nurture those relationships and to let these dear ones know I love them. My priorities have changed. An impromptu walk with a friend is more important than a clean house. I am a better listener; the advice giving is now secondary to the listening ear. I think I am more of an in-touch person than before. And, I would not be sharing these thoughts with you and reaching out to you if I had not experienced this grief.

7. Keep a sense of humor. I think the sense of humor has helped me keep my (sometimes doubtful) sanity. As terrible as death is, as awful as it is to lose someone, you can still find funny moments and events. As the cliché goes, "If you don't laugh about it, you will cry." For example, the first Lenten season after John died, someone asked me what I was going to give up for Lent. I replied, "Sex." First, there was this astonished look on the face, then laughter. I have photos on my refrigerator door. A friend inquired about each person and asked, "Where does your mother live?" I replied, "In the cemetery." He was stunned, then grinned from ear to ear. He said, "That's a good one. I'm going to have to

remember that for questions about my dad." A sense of humor puts others at ease. The deceased was human, and it is healthy to laugh about their antics and aggravations. Also, stress and tension subside if you can find some humor in the situation.

8. Refrain from despair. New events and challenges will come your way. Look upon them as something exciting, not as another burden. The world will never be the same to you as it was before your loved one died; but, your attitude will determine how quickly and how well you will adapt to your new situation. Have hope. Be patient. You will live again. A widow friend of mine told me, "You can have a good life. It is different, but it can be good." It is going to depend on you and your attitude.

9. Accept. As previously mentioned, after a while, I realized I was not grieving for John, per se, I was grieving for me. I was grieving for all the changes in my life and all I had to deal with. And let's face it, you really have to deal with all the issues yourself. You may have a support group, but it is ultimately up to you to *DO*. I was grieving and feeling sorry for *ME!* Then I realized that no matter what I did, I could not bring John back, and I could not make things "right" again. The only thing I could do something about was **me**, and once I made up my mind about this, my mind became clearer and my soul was at greater peace.

10. Live each day to the fullest. Putting off until tomorrow may be too late.

11. Be patient. Patience is truly a virtue, and time is your good friend.

If you are reading this before you have experienced grief, you should think *NOW* what you would do if left alone. Start making plans so that you will not feel like a cork out in the middle of the ocean.

I certainly do not know what curve balls life is going to throw me. But to quote from a friend's email, "We live in the real world, and in the real world, bad things can happen to good people. And it gets us down. People like you, and, I think, myself, don't stay down because we are too stubborn or too strong or sometimes even too foolish to know we can't do whatever we are trying to do. That doesn't mean we always come out on top, but we keep moving ahead. It also doesn't mean that when we are down the pain doesn't hurt. It does." Whatever happens, my feet are firmly planted, and I truly feel new doors will continue to open. My life is being re-created daily. Won't it be exciting to finally see the new me?

13

Summary

As with any experience, there are many lessons to be learned in grief. This walk through grief has definitely been the hardest and most thought provoking experience of my life. For the first time, I have come to the full realization of the power and pain of grief. In the depths of my being, I discovered emotions of such intensity it astonished me. I know I loved deeply, but I had no idea what other emotions lay lurking inside. Sorting through this explosion of feelings has been difficult and anguishing, as I am sure you realized if you have read each chapter of this book. Intellectually, I know that in each day there are thousands dealing with these same hurts, pains, and conflicts. Emotionally, I feel I am the only one.

How true it is, I do not know, but I have read that the grief suffered is in proportion to the love. That is, if one loves deeply, the grief will be long and deep. If one loves only minimally, then the grief will be short and not so intense. All I know is that my grief has been both long and intense.

The grief experience has made me more conscious of the opposites of life—birth and death, sickness and health, happiness and grief. Why the world was designed this way, I do not know. There are times I certainly do not approve of this design! Perhaps this design's purpose is to make us more appreciative and thankful for the good side when we experience the opposing bad side. The key is to keep a balance. Too far in either direction makes life boring, unhealthy, and sometimes even dangerous. Too much of the "good life" can result in apathy, complacency, and self-centeredness.

Among all the opposites are a beginning and an end. Sometimes these occur simultaneously, as with John's death. It was the end of my life as a couple and the beginning of my life as a person alone, forging a new identity. Sometimes my steps are forward, and sometimes I go backwards. Sometimes the steps are freely taken, and sometimes I am dragged kicking and screaming in a new direction.

In all this, I have learned that the deceased's journey is one of death, but your journey is one of life. It is up to you to make your life as productive and pleasant as you possibly can. And to all of us supporting others, we need to remember that unconditional love goes a long way in healing our souls and our world.

You will survive the grief. It takes fortitude, patience, love, support, grit, and faith. Just as the sun sets, it also rises. However, dark as the days, there is hope. You can do it! You must do it! By the grace of God you will do it! Peace be yours.

"You don't get to choose how you are going to die or when. You can only decide how you're going to live." Joan Baez

Appendix A

Living Will

A Living Will is a document that allows you to decide what should or should not be done to you in case you become incapacitated or terminally ill. A more extensive version is called an "Advance Directive of Health Care." With either of these documents, you can determine, before the need arises, whether or not you want to be placed on life support, receive tube feedings, be resuscitated, have major surgery or blood transfusions, and so forth. Though you can make specific statements regarding organ donations, it is best for you to sign a separate organ donation card if you would like to be an organ donor. Many states include a signature line for organ donations on the driver's license.

When you have signed your Living Will and/or organ donor card (in front of witnesses), be sure to discuss your wishes with and provide copies of the documents to your family and physician. Taking care of this matter beforehand should prevent your loved ones from having to make these difficult decisions during a stressful and emotional time. The document is of little use if your family does not agree with your wishes. Make sure they and your doctor clearly understand your wishes.

Following you will find a copy of my Living Will. Because state laws vary, it is best to ask your attorney, the state attorney general's office, physician, or the local hospital for a blank copy of the Living Will for you to sign. I am also an organ donor, and have indicated such on my driver's license and have informed my family of my wishes.

ALABAMA

DECLARATION

Declaration made this __3nd__ day of __April, 1990__ (month, year).

I, __Clara Ruth Hayman__, being of sound mind, willfully and voluntarily make known my desires that my dying shall not be artificially prolonged under the circumstances set forth below, and do hereby declare:

If at any time I should have an incurable injury, disease, or illness certified to be a terminal condition by two physicians who have personally examined me, one of whom shall be my attending physician, and the physicians have determined that my death will occur whether or not life-sustaining procedures are utilized and where the application of life-sustaining procedures would serve only to artificially prolong the dying process, I direct that such procedures be withheld or withdrawn, and that I be permitted to die naturally with only the administration of medication or the performance of any medical procedure deemed necessary to provide me with comfort care.

Other directions: _I wish to be kept informed of all happenings and to make my own decisions as long as I am capable._

In the absence of my ability to give directions regarding the use of such life-sustaining procedures, it is my intention that this declaration shall be honored by my family and physician(s) as the final expression of my legal right to refuse medical or surgical treatment and accept the consequences from such refusal.

I understand the full import of this declaration and I am emotionally and mentally competent to make this declaration.

Signed __Clara Ruth Hayman__

City, County and State of Residence __Dothan, Houston County, Alabama.__

The declarant has been personally known to me and I believe him or her to be of sound mind. I did not sign the declarant's signature above for or at the direction of the declarant. I am not related to the declarant by blood or marriage, entitled to any portion of the estate of the declarant according to the laws of intestate succession or under any will of declarant or codicil thereto, or directly financially responsible for declarant's medical care.

Witness _Dawn Cooley_

Witness _____

Courtesy of Society for the Right to Die, 250 West 57 Street, New York, NY 10107.

Appendix B

Checklist

When a death occurs, there are many decisions that are made in haste, made during a time of confusion, or are made under great emotional strain when one is most vulnerable. Most wrong decisions can be avoided if preparations are made and discussed before a death occurs.

The following is a checklist of items that should be filed together in a special place in your home so they are easily accessible when needed. It is advisable a copy be kept in a safe deposit box and/or another place of safekeeping. Remember that a safe deposit box is unavailable after business hours and on weekends. At least two persons need to be familiar with these items and where they are stored. Information should be updated on a regular basis.

- ☐ 1. List of persons who should be notified upon your death. Include their mailing address and their telephone number.
- ☐ 2. Clergy's name, address, and telephone number.
- ☐ 3. Physician(s)' name, address, and telephone number.
- ☐ 4. Dentist's name, address, and telephone number.
- ☐ 5. Attorney's name, address, and telephone number.
- ☐ 6. Accountant's name, address, and telephone number.
- ☐ 7. Name, address, and telephone number of the funeral home where the body should be taken.
- ☐ 8. Name of cemetery, its location, the cemetery lot number and certificate number (if applicable), and the telephone number of the contact party where the interment should take place. If

cremation is desired, there should be specific instructions indicating this and instructions as to where to place the ashes. Please discuss this method of burial with family members so they know your wishes. It is very important that you make a decision now as to where you want to be buried. If cemetery lots need to be purchased, do it NOW. Do not wait until death occurs; this just adds a burden on your loved one. As unpleasant as the thoughts are in facing your own mortality and taking care of these matters, it is of utmost importance you take care of this business now. It is also advisable that headstones be purchased. They can be placed at the gravesite. They do not have to be engraved until after death occurs. It is advisable that the family name be placed on the stone in order to mark the gravesites and to keep someone else from claiming the stone.

☐ 9. Any special instructions concerning your funeral service including: music; Scripture reading; names of pall bearers; flowers; type and monetary limitations on the casket and vault; and, burial clothes.

☐ 10. Burial policy, including the name, address, and telephone number of the contact person.

☐ 11. Any instructions concerning the obituary. A lot of people prewrite their obituary and keep it updated.

☐ 12. Name, address, telephone number, contact person, and account numbers of bank accounts, savings accounts, treasury notes, and stocks/securities.

☐ 13. Name, account number, and contact number for credit cards. It is recommended that you keep in your file a photocopy of each of your credit cards with the number to call.

☐ 14. Name and address of bank, box number, list of inventory, and location of the key for safe deposit box(es).

☐ 15. Information about yourself, your spouse, and your children:
- Full, legal name (include maiden name when appropriate)
- Birth date
- Birthplace

- Parent's name(s) and birthplace(s)
- Social Security Number
- Religious affiliation
- Birth Certificate
- Marriage Certificate
- Passport
- Armed Services discharge papers, if applicable
- Adoption papers, if applicable
- Divorce papers, if applicable

☐ 16. Will. Everyone needs a will. If you die without having one, it is called dying "in testate" which means the state determines how your property is divided. A will should include: who gets custody of your children if they are under age and what financial provisions you have made for them; person whom you desire to be the executor of your estate; and, how to handle any outstanding debts. Be sure to consult with an attorney in writing a will. Please note that the beneficiaries listed on insurance policies, securities, and such SUPERSEDE the wishes of a will. So, it is important that you and the attorney make sure that ALL papers are in order and everything is consistent with your wishes. Also note that the spouse does not automatically inherit all the assets from the deceased spouse. If there is no will, most state laws give the surviving spouse only one-third to one-half of the estate with the remainder going to the children. Parents and siblings will get the balance if there are no children.

☐ 17. Durable Power of Attorney, which designates a person to take control of your financial affairs in case you become incapacitated.

☐ 18. Information pertaining to a Trust.

☐ 19. Lists of any outstanding debts (including any contracts and mortgages) with the name, address, telephone number of the contact person, and any supporting account numbers.

☐ 20. Business records and the name, address, and telephone number of any contact persons.

☐ 21. All deeds and/or titles to any property, including house, cemetery plot, automobiles and other property.

☐ 22. Any receipts and/or appraisals of valuables, including antiques and jewelry.

☐ 23. Insurance policies (car, medical, property, life, accident, etc.) along with the name, address, and telephone number of the contact person for each policy. Make sure the desired beneficiary is designated in the policy. Remember that the designated beneficiary is the one who will get the money, even if you specify someone different in the will.

☐ 24. Folder of armed services information, including the Service Serial Number and the discharge papers. If eligible, the Veterans Administration may help pay the funeral/burial expenses, provide a flag to drape over the casket, and provide a headstone.

☐ 25. List of memberships and organizations to which each member of your family belongs. Include membership numbers, addresses, and contact information.

☐ 26. Any papers concerning any pension plans and IRAs.

☐ 27. Copies of the most recently filed Federal and State Taxes.

Appendix C

Notes on Financial Matters:

1. Be sure to maintain good financial records.
2. Maintain an up-to-date list of financial assets.
3. Explore now, and know the financial consequences of survivor benefits of any IRAs and annuities you hold.
4. Always discuss with your spouse or other family member the family's financial status.
5. Spend the extra and get the advice of an estate attorney, especially if you feel your estate will be subject to estate taxes. A few hundred dollars spent now may save thousands in the future.
6. Make copies of EVERYTHING and store them in a safe place.
7. It is advisable that funeral expenses be explored and decided upon. It is wise to place cost limitations on these expenses. Large funeral debts are often incurred by making decisions under duress.
8. Though it sounds trite today, be sure that you know how to balance the checkbook.
9. Remember, taking time now to get things in order will make a difficult time easier for the survivor(s).

Appendix D

What to Do When Death Occurs

At the time of death

Following is a checklist of what to do when a death actually occurs. The funeral director should help with many of these arrangements, but the extent of the help depends on the availability of their staff, the services offered, and the costs involved.

☐ 1. If the death occurs at a medical facility, inform them of where the body should be taken for preparation for burial. If the death occurs at home, call the family physician and make arrangements from there. Inform the medical facility if the deceased is an organ donor.

☐ 2. Notify family and friends.

☐ 3. Call the appropriate clergy. If you do not have one, the funeral director should be able to help with this.

☐ 4. Contact the funeral home and make an appointment to select the casket, vault, determine the date/hour of service, type of service, funeral transportation, and other arrangements. Note that the funeral director should be responsible for securing the necessary burial permits and death certificates. Be sure to inform the funeral director if cremation is desired. The funeral director will know the laws pertaining to the cremation process and the disposal of the ashes. If the deceased is to be sent to a distant point for a funeral and/or burial, the funeral director will also make those arrangements.

☐ 5. Write the obituary and funeral notices. Usually the funeral home will be responsible for placing these in the designated newspapers.

☐ 6. Make arrangements for the six pallbearers, any honorary pall-bearers, and for the music.

☐ 7. Go to the florist and select flowers to go on top of the casket and any other floral arrangements needed. Do not forget the boutonnières for the clergy, musicians, and pallbearers. If chari-table donations are desired in lieu of flowers, make sure the funeral home knows this, and include it in the obituary.

☐ 8. Determine the amount of honorarium for the clergy and musi-cians, get cash, and place each honorarium in an envelope and label with the person's name.

☐ 9. Notify the attorney of the death.

☐ 10. Take the following with you when you meet for your appoint-ment with the funeral director:
- Burial clothes—take socks, underwear, suit, and tie for men; take hose, underwear, dress, jewelry for women.
- Birth certificate of the deceased.
- Social Security Number of the deceased.
- Military discharge papers.
- Burial policy. If funeral arrangements have been prepaid, bring along the receipts and other pertinent papers.
- Insurance claims forms, for notification purposes.
- Names of clergy and pallbearers.

☐ 11. Determine how many copies of the death certificate are needed. The funeral home usually makes arrangements for these to be sent to you. For most business transactions, a *certified* copy of the death certificate is needed, which means you cannot make copies. It is a good idea to determine before death occurs what business transactions will require a death certificate so that you will not be at a loss when asked how many you need. It is better to have too many than to run out and have to make arrange-ments to get extras.

☐ 12. Have notepads and pens readily available to record telephone calls received, food received, flowers, and other acts of kindness so that you can write thank you notes at a later date. Instruct family members and friends to keep this list updated. Unless you keep a running list, it will be easy to forget someone's act of kindness.

After the funeral

There are many areas of business that need to be taken care of after the death of a loved one. Below is a checklist to help you to remember what needs to be done. As each item of business is taken care of, make notes of what was done, the date the business was handled, the person you dealt with, and any other notes that might be useful to you in the future. Whether or not you realize it, your mind is "foggy" and concentrating and remembering details are very difficult. So, keep a pad and pen handy, and write down any and all information.

☐ 1. Contact the attorney. Have the attorney start the probate process for the will. Probate is the process of proving the validity of a will before an estate can be distributed to the rightful heirs.

☐ 2. Contact the accountant.

☐ 3. Notify and change ownership, if applicable:
  • Banks / stocks / bonds / securities / treasury notes / IRAs / annuities
  • Safe deposit boxes
  • Credit card companies
  • Utility companies (gas, electric, telephone, water, sewer, etc.)
  • Department of Motor Vehicles
  • Subscriptions
  • Any organization where the deceased was a member
  • Companies where the deceased had a pension fund
  • Mortgage companies
  • Insurance companies

☐ 4. Obtain copies of the death certificate

- ☐ 5. Contact the Veterans Administration if the deceased had military service.
- ☐ 6. Contact the Social Security Administration. Be sure to have the Social Security telephone number available beforehand.
- ☐ 7. Contact any Union or Fraternal organizations.
- ☐ 8. Contact all insurance companies (car, house, medical, life, etc.)
- ☐ 9. Contact the banks and any other financial institutions (savings and loans, brokerage houses, etc.)
- ☐ 10. Contact any lending institutions where the deceased had any type of mortgage or loan.
- ☐ 11. Contact any organization where there is a retirement or pension plan.
- ☐ 12. Make sure the funeral director provides an itemized bill of all expenses incurred.
- ☐ 13. Pay funeral expenses, medical expenses, and other bills that are due.
- ☐ 14. Clean flowers off of grave, if this service is not provided.
- ☐ 15. Return food dishes.
- ☐ 16. Write thank you notes to clergy, musicians, pallbearers, people who brought food, sent flowers, made charitable donations, and did other acts of kindness.

Resources

There are many additional resources that address the various issues of grief. You should consult your local library or bookstore. Following are four small books and some resources that you might find helpful.

Claypool, John. *Mending the Heart.* Boston: Cowley Publications. 1999.

Katafiasz, Karen. *Finding Your Way Through Grief.* St. Meinrad, IN: Abbey Press. 1995.

Lewis, C. S. *A Grief Observed.* New York: HarperCollins Publishers. 1961.

Westberg, Granger. *Good Grief.* Philadelphia: Fortress Press. 1971. (Recently reprinted)

Check with your local Hospice program for help and materials or access them through www.hospice-america.org

AARP provides both legal advice and grief support. Contact them at www.aarp.org

For counseling, contact the American Counseling Association at 800-347-6647.

Ordering Information

Additional copies of the book may be ordered by contacting:

MBF Press
105 South Court Street
Montgomery, AL 36104
toll free: (866) 639-7688 • info@mbfpress.com
www.mbfpress.com/walkthroughdarkness

The cost is $12.95 per book, plus $6.95 shipping.

Ms. Hayman is also available for speaking engagements and for conducting grief seminars.

Please inquire regarding *Shooting for the Stars,* a life planning growth book, a companion volume to *A Walk Through Darkness.*

www.ingramcontent.com/pod-product-compliance
Lightning Source LLC
LaVergne TN
LVHW011412080426
835511LV00005B/496